I0142904

NEITHER HERE NOR THERE

Poems

Thomas Grissom

NEITHER HERE NOR THERE

Poems

SUNSTONE
PRESS

SANTA FE

© 2011 by Thomas Grissom. All Rights Reserved.

No part of this book may be reproduced in any form or by any electronic or
mechanical means including information storage and retrieval systems without
permission in writing from the publisher, except by a reviewer
who may quote brief passages in a review.

Sunstone books may be purchased for educational, business, or sales promotional
use. For information please write: Special Markets Department,
Sunstone Press, P.O. Box 2321, Santa Fe, New Mexico 87504-2321.

Book and Cover design ▸ Vicki Ahl
Body typeface ▸ Constantia
Printed on acid free paper

Library of Congress Cataloging-in-Publication Data

Grissom, Thomas, 1940-
Neither here nor there : poems / by Thomas Grissom.
p. cm.
ISBN 978-0-86534-839-4 (pbk. : alk. paper)
I. Title.
PS3607.R577N45 2012
811'.6--dc23

2011035928

WWW.SUNSTONEPRESS.COM
SUNSTONE PRESS / POST OFFICE BOX 2321 / SANTA FE, NM 87504-2321 /USA
(505) 988-4418 / ORDERS ONLY (800) 243-5644 / FAX (505) 988-1025

For Tom and Karen and Stone

Contents

Neither Here nor There

A line here, a line there
Words stitched together 'most anywhere
As if what's said must keep apace
Though not be bound to any place
But left unfettered free to roam
'Till in due time they find a home
As thoughts of universal truth—
For which time, not place, is the only proof.

Order Out of Chaos

The witless winds of wisdom scour the land
And pile debris haphazard in old fence corners:

Turn not your back on the disorder of the world
Printed on the pages of discarded newspapers

Shun not the delicate details of detritus
Marooned in abandoned mounds of middens;

Plastered to the earth in rain-soaked sheets
Long forgotten news may yet make sense

Heaped in some remote out of the way place
Even a pile of junk may have left some trace.

Trout Are Philosophers

A single line
written
on a scrap of paper hastily

abbreviated
by a momentary but fleeting clarity
one

of many thoughts that come
and go
like fish trailing flies

the world spinning
on beyond the meaning
long ago

forgotten
trout are philosophers
it said

then
and still does now
though

neither they
nor I
nor the spinning world know why.

Poems by—

I like the style, his technique—
No, really; I do—
The clever cryptic choice of words
The sudden surprising twist and turn,
The unanticipated image—trouble is,
I don't know what the hell he is saying
Half the time—then what is there
To like? It is poetry isn't it,
Or merely one more empty riddle
To nothing new under the sun?
I don't want my poetry
To be something I have to study—
Damn it man, could it be the fault
Is not entirely mine?

The Best of John Prine

There we were at the Tacoma Dome
With maybe twenty thousand other folks
All jammed too close together, into cheap plastic seats—
Mostly facing the wrong way,
Too far back to see—

And the loud speaker—
Reminding you that drinking is permitted
Only in the lounge
And smoking's not allowed,
And they probably don't want you to fart, either

And up there on the stage
Ol' John Prine
Singing "Angel from Montgomery"
And "It's a Big Old Goofy World"—
Sippin' on a drink between songs,
Smoking a cigarette,
And probably farting too, if he got the urge.

William Tell

I placed on his youthful head, trusting,
Even eager, whose face across the empty years
I can no longer recall beyond the vaguest notion
And yet the most specific recollection

The empty cardboard box—cylindrical, tall,
With its figure of a smiling Quaker
Whose broad beaming countenance
Replaces in the dark light of memory
His own forgotten face,
But whose pacific smile could not shield
Against the sure swift flight
Of my arrow

And plotted my purpose:
To lay at his feet
In the burning sun and choking dust
That empty box impaled upon my shaft,
The deed likewise impaled forever in fame
And spirit, soaring and yearning
By that one act of youthful daring
To finally escape that place;
Then stepped off one pace for each
Of the fingers on those two hands
That would do the deed

And drew the bow,
Its graceful limbs bent
Like the crescent of a new moon
Replacing now that blinding sun
In my dream haunted sleep,
Recalling his eyes
Held tightly closed
The way I had instructed
That he might not move and spoil the shot

Or worse. And feeling
The linen cord cutting deeply
Across the three last digits,
And taut muscles holding back the strong string,
Aimed at the static smiling face
Six inches above that pale flat space
Between his closed eyes

And shot.
The shaft a blurred streak of light
Glistening in the sun
Stood Zeno-like in that intervening space
And hummed its indifferent song
The air vibrant with the danger
Of its choice, yet
Unerringly seeking out the pacific countenance
To spare that other faceless one
And keep my hopes,

And his, alive.
The dust in little puffs spurted
As the fallen box and smiling face
Danced, squirming, on its feathered axis
About that plain bare space between us,
As it does still
In my dream disturbed slumbers

Then came to rest.
And he willing, even eager,
To face again the flying shaft
And see this time
The deed done that I would never do,
Could never do again,
Who, in spirit soaring and yearning
To finally escape that place
Gambled all on that one shot

And lost. Held fast
By that other nameless one
Whose face across the empty years
I can no longer recall beyond the vaguest notion
And yet the most specific recollection,
Impaled like that broad smiling countenance
Lying motionless in the dust,
Bound forever in deed and memory
To that never forgotten place.

Midnight Sun

We met above the Arctic Circle, in
Inuvik, Northwest Territories, no
Road farther north. We had something in common:
He was a German, without prejudices
He said, from Dortmund, and knew the elder Von Braun;
I was a physicist up from the South,
Also without prejudices, I told him,
And knew the son. Once a roofer, he liked
To say he looked down on people, and owned
A hotel and a place in Edmonton
Another one in Acapulco. He
Enjoyed talking with physicists, he said,
Especially one who knew a student of Sommerfeld's
And so we passed the time. He talked freely
About himself, I listened to his story.
A Hitler Youth, mining in the Cassiar Range,
Mushrooms in Edmonton, and now this, the finest
Hotel in the Arctic, a millionaire twice over
And self-made, with all the usual complaints
About how things are now. He showed me the three
Bars, the grand ballroom, he had built it all
With his own hands. Three floors completed and two
More planned when the beautiful Brunhilde
(That is what he called her) had ordered him
To stop. "She is so beautiful," he told me with
A twinkle in his steel gray eyes, "but oh,
So brutal. What brings you to the North?"
"Wilderness," I answered, "and because I have never

Seen it." "Wilderness," he scoffed. "Then say for
The sake of space and solitude," I offered instead.
He was not easily put off, "I have had
Too much of space and solitude for one life,"
He said. "Solitude is merely something you think
You want only when you don't have it. Men
Were not meant to be alone but together.
This hotel full of people is all the solitude
I want," he said, "and what good is all that space
When there's nothing here to put in it? Ah,
But for my part, I wish I could sell the frigging
Place and get the hell out," he confessed.
I might have accused him that he had both—
Yet seemed to want neither, but it
Would not have been an act of kindness
Befitting his place as host. Afterwards
I made my way back to my camp and my tent,
He to catch a plane to Edmonton.
We each had come our different ways to be here,
I thought, and had something more in common.
The sun wouldn't set at all that night, but from our
Different directions the world was closing in on us.

Augury

There are dark forces about
O Lords and Ladies
They walk the wide earth with impunity
And reach to the very bounds of heaven
And can be seen long afterwards
In a severed chicken's neck.

Questions

Paniak, O Paniak
Where are you gone?
Empty villages, silent tundra slopes—
Scrimshaw and dolls in curio shops:
Ishi was too gentle
But you—
Could it be you
Were too wise?

What

What is there to write?
That the earth is not flat
But round
And the sun neither sets nor rises
But the shining earth, swimming in its light,
Turns steadily toward it?

This is no longer the new world—
Nor yet the old—
And can never again be either.

Facts, once confronted
Soon run their course, give way
To thoughts, and we are left
With that which has never been written:
The mystery behind the facts—
I only began to live my life
When I knew it was going to end.

Reverie

The
moment; Augenblick
arrested

—immersion—

past severed
future's never
thoughts irrevere—

suspended at the nadir
propelled backwards
and forward
together...

Ah, yes, I see...

Dilemma

We are here for only a brief time
To experience and enjoy what will be here
For only a short while longer;
It is our overwhelming sense of wonder
That gives us our most distinguishing characteristic:
That bestows the pleasures of our enjoyment
And exacts the painful price of our finitude.

False Starts

—"You don't sound like a scientist,"
he said to me—
"Good," I thought.

On the desk
Ehrenfeld's
The Arrogance of Humanism:
In it the bookmark—
A lottery ticket.

Nothing now is left
Of the tiny thicket beside the house,
Except my too long story
About the woman and the fawn
And the solitary inscrutable old dog.

Tellers of Truth

Some few poems. Once I dared to think it possible
And spoke my mind freely, if brashly and without grace;
But how does one become what one is not? Now
At last perhaps I am ready, nothing left to lose and no
Pretense, just honesty without rancor and yet in everything
Some good if anything at all. It may yet be possible,
Those few left off a new voice may emerge guided
By an uncompromising regard and the need to find
Some truth. About that I am not as confident
Or as convinced as I once was, but clearer eyed
And better able to judge. We need honest poets,
Tellers of truth, not painters of pretty pictures.

Blank Verse

A blank sheet of paper
Lifted carefully, reverently, from a stack of blank sheets
Too numerous and overwhelming to contemplate
Intimidates me with its blankness;
Unmarked by ruled lines or anything restricting or confining
Its blankness silences me,
Its unblemished whiteness and purity inhibit me;
It is simple enough to put into words some initial thought
Just to get started,
Never the right one or, if close, not the right words,
Lined through or erased some mark or smudge remains
Informing me of failure, casting a pall over the page
And over my thoughts—I am like the artist sketching who
Erases everything attempted for the first couple of hours
Until finally hitting his stride he takes off
And continues undeterred by the blankness and want
Of what he—and I—have yet to do;
The words when at last they do come are never enough
To fill the daunting blankness,
There must, you see, be a certain number of lines
All the blank spaces and silences filled in the proper order
To build the structure,
Where even then there remain the blank spaces and silences
Between the words—and between the lines—that go unfilled, there
The real meaning of the poem takes refuge
Hiding still in the unfilled blankness and silence.

Jeffers Redux

That the age will decline, civilizations crumble, and man turn murderous
Is true enough, but mostly irrelevant. That hawk and rock and windswept wave
Are symbols of the natural beauty of things is true also, but a truth that bestows
No salvation. These truths are powerless against the necessity of life, impotent
Against the need for man to act. Not mountains nor desert nor the trans-human
    beauty,
But man, is the measure of things: Lacking man's consciousness—the inward eye
Turned outward—the universe is but mindless matter, devoid of beauty or meaning.
That things are beautiful we do not need great poets to tell us: beauty is printed
    plainly
On each man's soul. That man deceives and betrays and is frequently deluded
Is nothing new. Yet hunger and desire and the need for shelter have created great
    civilizations;
Curiosity and insatiable craving for answers, great discoveries; passion and yearning,
Great music, art, and poetry. These too are beautiful: man is part of the beauty.
These things we do not need great poets to tell us: Not *how*
But *why*: the vast unquenchable mystery of why.

All Is Mystery

These things we know:
That the universe is expanding
That it has been for a long time
That it may continue to expand forever,
That stars form galaxies and galaxies clusters and they in turn
Clusters of clusters on a scale unimaginable,
That the elements are formed from hydrogen and helium in the furnace of the
       stars
Spewed throughout the cosmos by the cataclysmic crescendo of a star's death
       throes,
That something earlier gave rise to hydrogen and helium,
That we who know these things are made from this same stardust—
But know little else besides,
Not what came before nor what will come afterward—
All but these few things are uncertain and shrouded in mystery.
The Pythagoreans believed all was number, Empedocles that love and strife
Brought all into being from earth, air, fire, and water; Leucippus thought
All was made of atoms and the void, for Plato it was the elusive Forms: for us
Electrons, photons, and quarks, and this too is surely doomed to failure;
For Heraclitus was right: Nature loves to hide, and the oracle
At Delphi neither speaks nor conceals, but gives signs: All is mystery.

The Co1smological Principle

Everywhere and in every direction
The same, except here
On this blue and white speck:
It required Copernicus, Kepler, Galileo, and Newton
To convince us that Aristotle and Ptolemy were wrong—
A legion of thinkers since
Have only deepened the mystery—
Wispy strands of matter swirl, compress, catch fire
And explode spewing stardust through the void and
We are the result: nowhere the same
Everywhere different, there is nothing else like us:
The mystery deepens, no cosmological principle
Can mask our difference amid the vastness
Of all this sameness, not Darwin surely
Or even a few strands of DNA, they are no better
Really than the older stories—
We just are, the beginning and the end,
Born of and returning to
The mystery.

The Vast Unquenchable Mystery

That there is no Christian God—how could there be?—scarcely needs saying,
No Islamic God or Hebrew God: none of the little narrow-eyed, human-hating
    gods—
Only the one undeniable God: the vast unquenchable mystery at the core of
    things.
Out of the mystery we emerged, and to it we return; between birth and death
    we harbor it
In our hearts, nurturing and worshipping it; or fearing and denying it
Seek solace in the countenance of these other grinning, gap-toothed gods.
It will not be denied. The mystery is beautiful but also terrible. Science
Disguises it in the tawdry cloak of description, answering *how* but never *why*
And, lately, even that scant little more sparingly. Our minds have played a trick
On us. With them we have probed the vast cosmos and the tiniest microcosm
Discovering at the heart of each the mystery our minds cannot know—
Reason stymied by itself. If there is *any* mystery, it is *all* mystery
And our questions all unanswerable, and that is both beautiful and terrible—
The choice is ours. Choose the God of mystery:
That way to make the beauty less terrible.

Unsimple Lies

I have had too much of God—and gods—
Invoked where they are powerless and impotent:
To explain what is unexplainable—
Or intruding where they are least welcome
And most harmful: to hide behind and alibi
What only humans can decide—though I confess
I much prefer the latter to the former: gods
To God—if any god is needed, surely
All are; the mystery of this world so far
Exceeds the bounds of any single God,
Or even a host of deities, we may as well
For all that heed Lucretius and dispense
With them completely for atoms and the void,
And rid ourselves of fear and superstition:
If by God we mean we cannot understand,
Leave it at that—more honest than to turn
That simple truth into such unsimple lies.

The Ancient Quarrel

Poetry is a sleight of hand—turning
One thing obscure into another clear—
Plato knew it, and early became the Master
Poet—when logic fails fall back upon
Metaphor and the power of language to persuade—
He most often did, and we love him for it.
Language is lovelier by far than logic
And more convincing too, the nature of the world
Makes certainty a gag while granting the existence
Of possibilities, the very art of poetry—
That's what the Poet in Plato understood:
Plato's arguments are fatally flawed
Any beginner can spot the errors—
The irony of Socrates to point them out—
But his instincts were true and pure
And we grant him the benefit of the doubt
Seduced by the sweetness of his rhetoric.
Plato the Philosopher quarreled with the Poets
Accusing them of lying about the gods
And banished them from the Republic—
The Poets—the Poets lie too much, mocked Nietzsche—
No, not lies, Plato, but a skillful sleight of hand
Turning one thing obscure into another clear:
The hard unavoidable truths—lacking which
Philosophy, Plato, is but a gilded web of deception.

Philosopher Poets

Camus didn't like the short poem—
Didn't understand it, I believe,
May have been the way he put it—
Nor the fleeting images by which meaning
Is compressed and conveyed in the cinema:
Brevity in the service of meaning was no virtue—
The philosopher in him preferred instead
The extended argument where one can tease
And probe an idea, exploring and drawing it out
Until its every sparkling facet shines smooth
And polished in the reflected light of reason,
All roughness and dullness dispelled—
One imagines Joseph Grand in *The Plague*, struggling
To find exactly the right words for his first sentence,
Who ends by saying nothing—
Yet *The Myth of Sisyphus* stands to *The Plague*
As a brilliant short poem to a longer epic:
The argument there turns nowhere on reason
Beyond the absence of it, relying on imagery and metaphor
To seduce and cajole and persuade, not unlike
Plato before him: Never state plainly in writing
Anything you actually believe, Plato wrote a friend,
Leaving us to approach him with that warning.
What goes unsaid is often the better part of each—
Where philosophy weaves its tangled webs
Simpler is better, less is more,
Philosophers become Poets.

De Rerum Natura

Do things truly move—and to what end—or is motion an illusion?
The Presocratics, no fools, bent on understanding the world wondered
        about it—
Heraclitus thought change was the nature of things:
Lacking motion, space and time—even matter—would be unintelligible
And the world cease to exist. Parmenides
Acknowledged appearances but looked for a deeper truth:
Behind appearances lay the reality of the One, complete and unchanging,
Unmovable and unmoving—compared to this truth the world
Of experience was illusory and misled our understanding;
Change meant something became what—or where—it was not
And Not Being, argued Parmenides, could not be conceived,
Only Being was conceivable—true reality admitted no change
No motion. The Pluralists worked a compromise, a synthesis
Between Heraclitus and Parmenides: they sought the unchanging
Many out of which appearances emerged: the earth, air, fire, and water
Of Empedocles from which Love and Strife created the harmony
And chaos of the world in constant warfare; the indestructible atoms
Of Lucretius swirling endlessly through the void, combining unseen
To form everything we see, in motions governed by the atomic swerve,
Or chance; to the oscillating electrons, photons and quarks that make up
        our world—
We have changed the details but not the story. It required Galileo
And Newton to set aside *why* and focus on *how* things move
And the laws of motion stood at once revealed. Now we have come
Full circle: the new physics equates matter and motion—
To exist it must move—and Heraclitus prevails: But to what end?
That path is the one Plato chose and philosophy has strode since. From

The new physics we know how motion proceeds in mounting detail
But why and to what end, or where it is leading us, we are no further along
Than the ancients. Neither physics nor philosophy can answer, only the
      poets:
Here be dragons and deep mystery and yes, great beauty, reassuring us
The world is worthwhile because it lies beyond understanding—
Only charlatans and fools presume to answer what cannot be answered—
What can be explained, said Yeats, is not poetry
And there the matter rests.

Confession

If by God you mean
Nature and the physical universe—
I am the most devout of acolytes;
If by it you mean anything beyond the mystery
And wonder of the present moment—
I am the most doubting of atheists.

Symmetry

There is a poetry of sadness, and a poetry of solace
And they are not different they are the same
The same song speaks both, and the same words—
The going away is but the coming again, and
Whatever is lost is what is gained. Along with these,
Also a third, a poetry of solitude and silence
And it too is not different, it too is the same—
In the solitude of sadness, the solace of silence—
In the silence of sadness, the solace of solitude:
In the silence of solitude and the solitude of silence
The refrains of sadness and solace sound the same.

The Baccae

It is a decided
defect
of the modern world

that
the quality of magic
is missing

It is for this
that we are seduced
by

tragedy
and believe
in evil.

The Sufferer and the Secret Cause

Did he ever read the words on the page
And wonder how on earth they came to be,
How from that diminutive boy whose laughter
He heard chase childhood into youth,
Turned suddenly quiet and serious,
Could erupt in bursts so unrestrained
Such depth of passion
Page after accumulating page,
Or was he by then too defeated
To even wonder—

Whether he had perhaps left too soon
While there was still some chance at redemption—
His if not the tormented young man's—
But cast away in the anger
And shame of failure
To leave him with only the agonizing questions
And amazement
At the mounting words on the pages
That by then had grown too numerous
To deny,
Staring back at him,
Contemptuously mocking his error—

And the young man—
Did the torrent of words make the loss more bearable
And sooth the hurt and rejection,
Or did they further divide and separate

And become in the silent depths of night
A bitter victory—

Did the long passage of time
Bring them peace and reconciliation,
Or merely deepen by its growing silence
The gulf between them
Until neither could fathom any way
To cross its treacherous depths—

Did the words on the printed pages
By which so many hearts have been united
With the sufferer and the secret cause
Become in turn the secret cause
That made sufferers of them both?

Conundrum

1st Premise:
> I don't belong here.

2nd Premise:
> But I am here.

3rd Premise:
> Conflicting premises
> need to be reconciled.

4th Premise:
> To reconcile is a verb.

5th Premise:
> Reconciliation lies in
> action or state of being.

Conclusion:
> 2nd Premise

Devotion

It must have been hard on her, possessing
Neither the kind of willful disregard nor the freedom of spirit
To throw off the prejudices of her day, lying there instead
Quietly in the dark while he groped and then
Found her through the many passionless nights
And the three children, waiting patiently for him
To finish and fall back because it was her duty—
Agreed to in the union of marriage but also out of
Feeling and genuine affection for him, unable to summon
The same dark desire or reckless abandon though
Awestruck and a little afraid of his, until finally
It ended in separate beds and then in separate rooms—
She relieved that it was at last over, he resigned
By then to let the embers of his youth cool and extinguish—
As though what they had become bore
No relation to what they once had been:
Let no one pity them the pleasures missed, the lost
Opportunity, not every star burns as brightly and all
Are cold and silent in that fathomless blackness:
Devotion was flame and heat intense enough for them.

The Meaning of Beauty

I recall thinking at the time
That she was not especially pretty,
She whose name I cannot now remember,
Though my memory of her, and then, is still as clear as ever.
I seem to recall—or imagine I do—
That her given name was Caroline
With the *i* pronounced long, the way it was then
And still is in the South, though of course
I would not have called her that—to me
She would have been Miss *"something I can't remember now"*
As the student-teacher in my high-school literature class—
We read Shakespeare that term, *Macbeth* and *Julius Caesar*.
She was married to an older acquaintance of mine
A towering, lumbering hulk of a young man
Whose shoulder and neck on one side were dished and scarred,
The result of surgery to remove lymph nodes for some reason,
Beside whose looming bulk and height her petite and diminutive form
Made a most incongruous, almost comical, pair.
His father knew Orville Wright and flew fighter aircraft in WWI
And was still flying crop dusters beyond seventy when
He was killed one evening in a crash. The son wrote poetry
Which he gave to me to read but I was too naïve
And inexperienced to understand or appreciate it
Though the three of us met sometimes to discuss it and talk
About literature and life, yet even there she was still my teacher.
They were optimists and believed literature possessed the power
To save the world; to me the world was less
A thing to be saved than accepted for what it is,

And I remember telling her so. I saw myself not as a participant
But an observer of life, remaining detached and aloof
Above the fray, making sense out of things not
By what people say, but by their actions and what they do:
Never mind their tears, just watch their hands.
Her green eyes flashing and long straight brown hair not done up
As in class but flowing freely about her neck and shoulders,
She bristled at the suggestion—the imagination that could
       conceive it,
She said, belies the whole idea, life can be understood only
By passionate immersion in the untidy messiness
Of human affairs, not as an objective observer—
I remember it still. She was suddenly alive and animated,
The plain round face and fierce narrow eyes blazing,
And I noticed her then in ways I had not before,
Even my friend took on a new aspect, as did the poetry,
Though I remember thinking at the time
That she was not especially pretty,
Back then when I was very young,
Before I understood the meaning of beauty.

In the Sweetness of Age

She lived across the street from me in a big
Two-story house with darkened, hollow-eyed windows
That always made me think of Faulkner's story,
"A Rose for Emily," though the house was not
Entombed in decay but well maintained
And newly painted white with green shutters,
And she was no spinster but well married
And for a year my high-school English teacher.
Her husband chaired the English Department at
The local college, collected Incunabula,
And played chess in the evenings by himself
Which left her with too much time alone for one
So wise and worldly. She chose her clothes to show
Her shape, not slender and little-girlish but full
And round and voluptuous, draped in soft
And clinging clothes that flowed across each curve
And contour to the very best effect.
She took a special interest in me, teacherly
At first, recommending writers and books
For me to read and providing copies from
Her own collection and her husband's library.
I was invited on occasion to discuss with him
The rare old books he collected, though in truth
I could never see what all the fuss was about.
Then later she would ask me over when
He was not there, in the afternoons
After school, to discuss what I was reading,
She said. Soon she was recommending all

The "best" novels, those with the "most explicit
And delicious passages," giving them to me
To read, and finally reading them to me
Herself during our afternoons together.
Her dress at first was proper but in time
Became more casual, until at last she wore
Only a robe fastened loosely about
The middle, and nothing else that I could tell.
As she moved about the room or took
Books from the shelf and leaned over me
I could see all that I was bold enough to dare.
She read the most erotic passages
With a coquettish, slatternly smile, her long
Brown hair, normally up, hanging down
In unkempt sprigs about her soft full face.
She showed me all the secret places in
The big old house, passages no longer used,
Closed up rooms, and inside one, darkened,
An unmade bed where she said she sometimes slept
Alone. I will not say now whether my hands
Found their way inside her robe that day
Or any other time, but my mind did
And my imagination, or whether we ever
Did make love together. Yet if so
Where is the harm now? None, by my reckoning,
Only good. She gave to me a gift, a fantasy,
And memories I shall always cherish
That sweeten, year by year, with age.

My Eulogy, Please

Although
Charles Bukowski
mentioned it first
he certainly
wasn't the first
to think it,
though neither
was I, an
honest sentiment
from his self-indulgent
self-centered bullshit
ranting, one
that I can
truly admire—

no eulogies, please—
no one
standing up to say:
"He was a great
guy, really..."
no pompous jerk
judging my worth
or lack of it
when it no longer
matters anyway

but a former lover
looking tastefully,
sedately slutty
someone perhaps
about whom they'll
wonder
What did he ever see
in her?
standing up to say:
"God, he was a really
great fuck...
I'm certainly going
to miss him..."

because she will
and because
with her
once or twice
I was.

Sacred Poems and Private Ejaculations

Her desiccated juices
crusted thin
upon the pendulous dangle

flakes and scales
at my coaxing grasp
to rain

upon the fallow floor
the detritus
of desire deprived

like the dandruff
of some itch
unscratched

why should we not
take things in hand
and write

in jetted streams
of alabaster
a more fitting finish?

Confirmation

A voice mocked: "God is dead."
"Liar, blasphemer," the People cried—
But that was all.
None, though they tried,
Could accost the speaker,
For none could determine from whence the voice.
Only "Liar, blasphemer," they clamored loudly—
And by their urgent cry of protest confirmed
What the secret scornful voice affirmed.

I Heard You

I have listened to your rant for years on the radio and television
Heard your empty threats and pointless promises
Seen your stern reproving scowls and false obsequious smiles
The two-mouthed talk of wrathful vengeance and all-redeeming love
The pathetic pleas for money—love gifts, I believe you call it—
To feed your greed and self-importance;
Seen you stage your miracle cures
Heard the inane foolish questions—
Tell us, Bill, how you came to know the Lord, or
Share with us, Jim, how you found Jesus—
Good god, people, no one knows the Lord unless he is deluded or
A fool or desperate beyond the point of endurance, and a wandering poet
Proclaimed himself the son of God, fancy that—
Listened to the absurd claims of Immaculate Conception
And virgin birth, miracles, the Resurrection and life everlasting;
Witnessed the silly, futile attempts to read the Bible literally—
I have read the Bible too: I love the language, which we owe
Not to any god but to King James' scholars and the English tongue,
And the stories, though there are too few for my taste
And the whole thing could use a good editor,
The refreshing smattering of philosophy in Ecclesiastes,
The tragedy of Job, though there one must heed Hemingway's advice
About Huckleberry Finn and stop reading before the end—
Everything after Job clasps his hand over his mouth and stands mute
Is just a cheap trick added later by a lesser writer—
Even Homer knew to stop with Hector's funeral—
Whenever I hear the whole ludicrous litany again I am reminded
Of something that came to me years ago as I was driving late at night

And listening to some radio evangelist: *Christians are so frivolous*—
Or more properly *Christianity* is so frivolous—
Except much older now, and wiser, and with more of an edge
I would put it into an entirely different idiom,
Because it isn't Christians only but all the world's religions,
All the crazy contrived cockamamie schemes to explain what
Everyone knows, deep down, can never be explained—
And anyway, who would want to live in a world that we could understand—
And why the hell does everyone keep looking the other way
And pretending the emperor is clothed when any child can see
He walks naked and ridiculous among men everywhere,
Except perhaps to be careful not to offend, and to keep from having to say
What I think every time I hear it all again:
You crazy goddamn fuckers.

Such Uncertain Certainty

And anyway who would want to live in a world
That we could understand? I wrote,
Then in a moment of sudden clarity realized,
Who indeed? That's the very problem, isn't it?
We insist on living in a world we think we understand
That's what world views are all about,
What all of history and philosophy consist of:
Seduced by ego or superstition, genius or madness—
Plato and Paul, Hegel and Nietzsche come to mind—
We have grand ideas and see visions, hear the voices of gods
Or become deluded,
Thinking we have grasped some profound truth or understanding
When we are no different really than the Greeks
Who saw Zeus or Hermes,
Athena or Apollo in the guise of a stranger beside the way.
We possess more sophisticated knowledge perhaps
But no greater understanding,
We still can explain nothing but a few facts in terms of other facts
Equally unexplainable,
We are certain of nothing beyond the depths and mystery
Of our own uncertainty:
Then spend our lives imposing our views on others and explaining
Why things do not work out the way they should have—
Tormented by our insecurities we persecute and punish those
Who do not see the world as we do, fearful we are wrong
And not wanting to have to confront that truth.
Better to embrace the mystery and celebrate the doubt
Than to live in a world made mad and murderous
By such uncertain certainty.

Great Foolishness

America is a place for great foolishness—
Grand gargantuan foolishness—
Glaring foolishness in religion, and politics, and public affairs,
Grinning one-hand-clasped-over-the-mouth foolishness
In private beliefs and public utterances,
Grave arrogant foolishness in making war:
Freedom we call it, the freedom for unbridled foolishness—
Where great latitude is granted, great folly is evident.
Foolishness itself is not foolishness
But a measure of license and liberty and tolerance:
The Greeks were a great people, confident and playfully foolish
The Poets sang of their greatness, Pericles spoke stirringly of it
The Philosophers strung it out for all time,
Yet Thucydides tells us how their great foolishness
Cost them their freedom and liberty and confidence—
In time, even their greatness—
Today they are but a memory, though an enduring one;
The Romans, determined to avoid the foolishness of the Greeks
Found new ways to be foolish, now they too
Are but a footnote to the memory of the Greeks;
Every age has been either cautious or foolish—
Our own as well—
Though none has learned how to be cautiously foolish
Or, failing that, foolishly cautious.
Our own foolishness has turned grim and ugly,
Too grievous by far to heed the lessons of past foolishness—
America is a place for great foolishness—
Someday they will speak of us in the same breath

With the Greeks and the Romans,
Only the scars we leave may be greater still
And even more foolish.

Citizens of the World

I am not a patriot
And I make no apologies
I do not spout empty slogans
Or hoist boisterous banners
I do not wave the flag
Or let it wave me
I do not pledge allegiance to a country
But to my principles
My allegiance is never granted
It must be earned and deserved
I am not stirred by martial music
Or glorious deeds in war and battle
War is never glorious
But degrading and demeaning
War is not winning
It is the final failure
I am not swayed by appeals to national pride
Or demonstrations of national power
But by justice and common decency
A nation is not a thing
It is the people
I am not a citizen of a country
But of the world
To those who would tout their patriotism
By pointing to others that threaten and kill
I understand the existence of evil
And the necessity to oppose it
Without becoming part of the evil itself

To those who seek my support
Let me hear first your reasons
Do not speak to me of patriotism
All you patriots:
I am not a patriot
And I make no apology.

Though I Would

I see people going to school
I'm glad I'm not
Takes away the time I could've had for learning
I see people going to work
I'm glad I'm not
Living day by day is now work enough for me
I see people going to church
I'm glad I'm not
I've no time left to waste that way
I see people shut indoors
I'm glad I'm not
Nature's bounds are the only walls I want
I see people marching in parades
I'm glad I'm not
That path too quickly leads to mischief
I see people waving flags
I'm glad I'm not
The time is better spent in talking
I see people going to war
I'm glad I'm not
Let those who want them fight the wars
I see people going to jail
I'm glad I'm not
Though I would
If the cause were right and just.

Such Sacrilege

God bless America? Perhaps. But why?
One hundred fifty years ago we were a nation
Of slaveholders, keeping an entire race of people
In bondage and chattel slavery. A nation divided
We fought a bloody and murderous war to resolve the issue
But didn't. For the next one hundred years both sides alike
Schemed and tricked and dissembled, and looked the other way
To deny justice and social equality to former slaves, freed
But never free. Nor was it that different for Asians and others of color
And those of religious and social distinctions: Native Americans,
Chinese, Japanese, Irish and Italians, Catholics and Protestants,
Hispanics, Latinos, Jews and Muslims, women and gays—the list has
         been writ
Many ways. God bless America? Perhaps. Yet evidently
Not all are blessed equally. One nation under God?
Such nonsense. Such rubbish and hypocrisy.

Let Things Change

Things change. Change is the nature of the world:
You can't step twice into the same river,
Said Heraclitus, and the physics of the twentieth century
Bears him out. At the quantum level motion endows existence
And nothing is ever at rest. We might have suspected it—
At rest with respect to what? We can find no answer.
Rest is merely an illusion of the slow-moving aggregate
World we live in. Even in it all things change.
I have grown older and have grown a beard. I no longer
Run as often or as fast and as far. The college where I taught
Has changed in ways that I find incompatible—
Time to move on. Before that I gave up what I was doing
Because it had come to seem wrong-headed and a mistaken direction.
More and more I deal with people who see the sagging features and the gray
      beard
And dismiss me as irrelevant. It doesn't bother me. They are reminding me
That I am coming to the end. Their time will come too.
Vanity of vanities, all is vanity
Said the Preacher, and he too was right.
Not even God stays the same. How many gods
By now have we had? If one of them doesn't do us in,
And we survive, there will be still others. They are as endless
As the fears that haunt our thoughts. God is our attempt
To find some constant by which to counter the changes
That confront us. Memory serves as well: I still go
In my mind to the scenes of my youth. So too does science
By making change at least law-bound. But now it isn't God
Or memory or science that interest me. At the end

Time speeds up and I become impatient to know
The outcome. Curb the gods. Unleash science.
Let things change. What is constant will out.

Let There Be Gods

In the stone tiles that line the walls of my shower
I see images, scenes in the golden brown earth tones
Of the desert, the leering faces of gods, the mystery of roiling clouds
Storm-wracked floods and chaotic battles peer out at me
From the stones. Am I so very different than the Greeks
Who saw the gods in everything around them—
In the shape of a bull or a swan, the goad of a stinging gadfly,
In the thickets and glens of Cithaeron, the stones of a wayside wall?
The Greeks were courageous and clear-eyed about the world:
If there were gods anywhere let them be everywhere
In all things, and face them squarely in every undertaking,
Anything less meant turning away from the world
And they meant to live fully, for now not later.
For that they required not *God* but *gods*; Zeus though supreme
Was neither omnipotent nor omniscient, over him
The chained Prometheus held sway and maintained the secret of his fate.
Their world was too complex and dangerous for any single god;
They faced its uncertainties piecemeal through many different gods,
And many different answers, posing them all against its various mysteries
Taking none too seriously—It is not at all certain,
Said Plato, what men actually think about the gods—
Relying ultimately on their own reason to guide them.
Our world too has lost its center, its unity lies shattered;
Big ideas no longer work, no single vision suffices
Philosophy and Science share Truth with the Poets
And we must face the dangers piecemeal, one by one.
For this, then, let there be gods: see them everywhere, in all things
Like the images peering at me from the stones of my shower.
Trust no one of them over the others, none over your own reason.

The Ways of Odysseus

I would not have made a very good Myrmidon,
One of Achilleus' fellows, sprung from ants
On the isle of Aegina in the reign of Aeacus,
Achilleus' grandfather. Fierce brave warriors like the ants
Zeus transformed to men, who followed Achilleus
From Peleus' Phthia to Priam's Phrygia and helped sack unfortunate Ilium.
Bent always on glorious deeds in war and battle
As their legacy, preferring a warrior's early death
With glory to a long and uneventful life
As the surest path to fame and immortality.
I am more inclined to the ways of Odysseus:
Not the sly seducer and "glib sharper" slandered as the son of Sisyphus,
But the wily tactician "skilled in all ways of contending"
Who won by wit and wile instead of the warrior's way.
To blinded Polyphemous he was "Nohbdy"
Who led his men to safety; to war-weary Achaeans
Exhausted by ten years of slaughter he was
The architect of the ruse that finally won the war,
Then by patient guile and cunning made his way ten years
Back to Ithaca to outwit and slay the suitors
And restore wife and hearth and home.
The world of Achilleus is without subtlety—
Die to be remembered is a fool's wager—
And without wonder and magic and mystery.
It was Odysseus that the Greeks remembered later
And admired most—the path of Athens over Sparta—
Preferring reason to sample the mystery and wonder
As the better prospect. Reason too may be only
A fool's wager, but a far, far sweeter one.

Trust No Abstraction

The real world is the one just outside my window
Not that one mirrored in the window of my mind:
The real world concrete, tangible, the object of experience
The other elusive, ephemeral, the product of imagination.
We so often confuse and jumble them: neither it seems is possible
Without the other, the only things real are matter and energy
And not knowing what either is we make them constructs of the mind,
Abstractions which we treat as though we knew; no
Conscious experience without the concept, about that at least
Kant was right; and no concept without the experience, about that
He was wrong. We easily interchange the one with the other
And so are led astray: we refine our abstractions to more nearly
Conform to the world we experience, then as quickly forget
They are but crude approximations, the best of them fall woefully short
Trust not what you are told, believe your own eyes;
The physicist's world is not the real world, nor can it ever be.
It is merely an abstraction, a beautiful set of equations
On a page, fertile lines and marks on a fecund sheet of paper,
Powerful and yet powerless, promising yet inadequate;
We fashion laws of motion to explain the collisions
Of billiard balls, the trajectory of stars and planets
Then are surprised when they cannot describe the motions of atoms.
The quest is never ending, what is omitted always exceeds
The little that can be included: no mystery, no magic
The Vast Unknowable, our intuition tells us—else
What is a God for. The real world is at our fingertips
Grasp it firmly, experience it fully: trust no abstraction.

The Philosophical Principle

I have looked into the eyes of the world's great philosophies
And seen them blink: where they try and go beyond experience
They are like the mindless babble of fools; where limited
To experience they are subservient and inferior to science;
It is only in human affairs that philosophy has its place,
About that Plato was certainly right, though, even there, too often
At the expense of evidence, of that Plato was certainly
Guilty: *The Prince* and *Leviathan* are as well supported as
Republic. There is only one true philosophical principle:
Believe nothing suggested solely by the mind, that great
Trickster and deceiver, and only a tiny portion of all the rest
And you will be right on occasion. The blood stained path
Of philosophy through history is strewn with the lack of
Evidence. We know only what we can observe ourselves
And at that we know but very little, only a miniscule portion
Of all we profess. For the rest we freely substitute belief,
The seductive but ignorant handmaiden of philosophy.
It is easier that way, and seemingly harmless, to ignore
The one philosophical principle: in the outcome of our beliefs
We risk only the fate of becoming its most convincing evidence.

The Beginning and the End

Thirteen and a half billion years ago—
Give or take for good measure a few billion or so—
The universe *erupted*: energy tightly pent-up in space-time abruptly
Expanding: not rushing *into* space, but powering the *expansion*
Of space and time itself: the Big Bang, the primordial fireball
The explosive, expansive, everywhere-outward rush of that initial eruption—
Metaphors that try to capture our understanding of it
But fall ever short. Built into the very physics that led us to discover it
Are intrinsic, inescapable limitations that render it powerless
To tell us the beginning; it remains an open question
Whether it can ever tell us the end. *The beginning and the end*:
They are among our earliest questions; our first stories attempt to answer them.
We are born, it seems, with some inkling of our beginnings,
Some hint of our ultimate destiny: *First of all*, said Hesiod, *there came Chaos,*
From Chaos was born Erebos, the dark, and black Night,
And from Night were Aether, light, and bright Hemera, the day, begotten
For Night lay in love with Erebos and conceived and bore these two;
In the beginning, says Genesis, *God created the heaven and the earth*
And the earth was without form, and void, and darkness was upon the face of the
    deep
And God said, Let there be light: and there was light
And God called the light Day, and the darkness he called Night. Our physics tells
    us
As the universe expands it cools. In the beginning the Big Bang would have
    been
Very hot, but dark and without form. As space-time expanded hot gamma rays
    cooled
Creating photons of visible light, transforming night into day

Though still an opaque universe, the photons of light trapped
By scattering from electrons and protons; expanding and cooling further
The scattering diminished, light was unleashed, the universe became visible;
Electrons combined with nuclei to make the first atoms—hydrogen, helium,
    lithium—
Creating order out of chaos; during the first few minutes the fireball
Was hot enough to fuse protons and neutrons into nuclei of helium and
    lithium,
All other elements formed later in the hot interior of stars, spewed forth
In the death throes of exploding supernovae: we are the resulting stardust;
It is fitting we retain some notion in our myths and stories. And what of the
    end
And our intuitions there? For now the expansion continues, the fate of the
    universe
In the balance: if gravity outweighs the energy of space, the expansion will halt
Then reverse, and the universe die in a fiery collapse, the very image of Hell
And Perdition. The Greeks had a different notion: Hades was the realm of
    shades
Land of the mournful dead wrapped in a gloomy solitude of eternal darkness
And desolation, life was a brief sweetness before everlasting death. Lately
We have found the expansion not slowing but accelerating, driven
By a mysterious energy overwhelming gravity, stretching the universe apart
Each galaxy left stranded in the darkness of its own isolation;
Perhaps ripping apart even the local bonds that bind galaxies
Banishing each cosmic speck to an eternity of bleak and barren solitude,
The blaze of the night sky only a brief sweetness before everlasting dark.
We will never know. We will have disappeared long before, our atoms scattered
On the cosmic winds. To the extent we are still part of the universe
It will be a world, it seems, of which we had once some inkling.

The Dawning of the Age

At the dawn of human consciousness
Homo sapiens was the center of the universe
If only because he was the center of his world:
How else could he be, how better to avoid the dangers
And secure his survival? Spirituality was the inner voice
At quiet times telling him he was right,
After all it was working wasn't it? There had to be
Some reason for it all, with him squarely at the center;
If there was any meaning to be found, it was himself
As the reason for all existence. The creation of gods
Was in his own likeness as well, by which
He made himself the object of the universe,
Then set about to conquer it with his mind.
Copernicus, Galileo, Kepler dislodged
The earth from its place at the center of things,
Newton made it unimpeachable. Now we know that
The sun is but one of a hundred billion stars in our galaxy
In a universe of a hundred billion such galaxies
And yet the worst was still to come: the stardust
Of which we and everything we can see is made
Is but a tiny fraction of all there is. The rest is still unknown:
We call it dark matter and dark energy
To mask our ignorance; but what we know
Is that it is slowly tearing the universe apart
Scattering the pieces on the cosmic winds. From
The center of the universe and the focus of gods,
To insignificant flotsam drifting among
The cosmic debris, we are truly insignificant

And inconsequential; we can no longer doubt it.
Yet we deny it still, as we should:
How else could we be, how else enjoy the fleeting moment
And the happy accident of our creation?

Being and Nothingness

Why is there anything at all? And if
Something, why *this* something and not *some other*?
Is it because, as the Eleatics believed,
There cannot be *nothing*; that Nothingness
Is only an illusion suggested by Being,
The way unicorns are suggested by horses?
But that does not explain *this* something. The only conclusion
Is that, if anything at all, then everything imaginable,
And our attempts to understand it are as futile
And unending as the endless variety conceivable,
And perhaps sometime, somewhere unicorns do exist.
Perhaps there is no all encompassing universe,
But a multi-verse of many parallel universes,
Each different in some respect from all the others
And language fails and must be expanded.
This idea by physicists was conceived to conceal
A profound embarrassment: the failure to reconcile
Quantum theory with cosmology, the extreme
Antipodes of our understanding; the one describing
A discrete microcosm of discontinuities, the other
A continuous cosmic mesh of smoothness. But it is not
Science, nevertheless, for no one can ever know—
What a theory allows is nowise demanded—
Merely a cunning conjecture by clever Poets
Dreaming idly of unicorns.

Epistemos

Science in the twentieth century has reshaped our view of the world
But mostly wrongly:
Not the oracle of certainty as was believed in the nineteenth century
But Prometheus bound
Chained and nailed to his rock, limited, his ambitions thwarted. Each
Advance in understanding paid for by an intrinsic limitation
In our ultimate knowledge of the world. Relativity imposes
The finite velocity of light as the limiting speed of our experience
Relegating knowledge always to the past. Quantum theory restricts
Determinism in the realm of the microcosm. Cosmology reveals
An ever-expanding universe accelerating toward complete emptiness.
Chaos theory describes a non-linear world deterministic
Yet inherently unpredictable. And like Prometheus
We find ourselves bound by chains forged from the links
Of our own cleverness
In uncovering the secrets of the universe. Only biology remains
A completely deterministic science, and only because it has yet
To discover its own ultimate truth.
Why did we think it otherwise? What the gods give they also
Take away.

Prometheus Bound

Prometheus bound: fettered and chained and nailed
To his rock at Zeus' bidding, and for what?
"I stopped mortals from foreseeing doom. I sowed
In them blind hopes." Prometheus, meaning foresight,
A god helping mortals and for it he was punished—
The human self-loathing that spawns religions:
We deem ourselves undeserving of help, even from
The gods. Is the story here the nature of the gods
Or about us and our obsession with guilt and shame?
"Besides, I myself gave them fire. From it
They will learn many useful crafts." And with it
Presumably also the bright light of illumination
And the hope of reason. Was that a blind hope
Against which the gods wished to protect us?
Is this a story about uncertainty in a world
Forever beyond our comprehension? Not even Zeus
Knew his own fate, though presumably Prometheus
Did, yet was unable to save even himself.
We have taken Prometheus' dare and sought our
Assurance of certainty in the knowledge of science,
Only to find it, too, fettered and chained and nailed
To the rock by the limits to knowledge: the finite
Speed of light, the indeterminism of quantum theory,
The unpredictability of non-linear chaos,
The accelerating expansion of the universe toward eventual
Emptiness. Those old stories of the poets ring true:
No certainty beyond the false assurances of religion.

Immortality

In my seventy years I have seen much of life
And bear its scars along with its fond memories
But for all that I would not prolong it forever.
Even the Greeks knew that immortality is a curse:
Achilleus chose wisely and we remember him today;
Those who lived forever among the gods had no further
Use of life. I can think of no age at which I would wish
To be suspended; those I might consider I remember
Fondly because they were fleeting and didn't last,
That would surely have spoiled them in the end.
It is its endless variety not its unending monotony
That gives life savor, we grow too soon tired of its boredom.
Prometheus was bound to his rock and Sisyphus was
Doomed to forever push his stone uphill and we pronounce
Them happy but mostly because we have no choice,
In them we see ourselves. We bear life because we believe
It will eventually end. And in that is our essential wisdom.
Life once experienced cannot be sustained without becoming
A burden and an immortal curse. The gods give in earnest
What we ask in jest. Perhaps it is only the voice of old age
But it is a warning to heed closely.

Montana Bound

Driving down the highway
In a fifth wheel rig named "Dreamer"
Listening to the music, the sad songs
That you gave me—New Orleans Katrina blues—
Eager with anticipation
Thinking the world is good, thinking life is grand
Wishing you were with me, glad that I knew you—
Our strides perfectly matched step by step together—
Wishing it were forever but grateful for the little while
Thinking life is good, wishing you were with me
Montana bound
Riding down the highway
In a fifth wheel rig named "Dreamer."

Voice from the Past

The phone rings
and the voice on the other end
speaks in soft Southern
accents

Mississippi, I tell myself—
patrician, stately, proper—
the Delta or the coast
not the hill country

not Alabama or Georgia
and not Carolina or Virginia—
Tennessee or Arkansas
Possibly—

each recognizably different
to an ear that grew up
immersed
in these sounds

this one I am fairly certain
is Mississippi
the accents still distinct and indelible
in my memories

reminding me
anew
that except for family and friends

these are voices
I turned my back on
years ago

not for relief from
the melodious sounds
but to escape
the harshness and hypocrisy

disguised
in soft Southern speech
the ideas and beliefs
I grew up with

but want no part of
and put aside

teaching myself to speak
like the voice
on the six o'clock news

learning to think conversing
with the voices found
in books

such a vastness
stretching
between then and
now

the voice on the other end
reminding me
tugging me toward
a past
I cannot escape

but am part of always
a past

I want to keep
forever
in the past,

I am sorry
I hear myself saying,

I am afraid
you have
the wrong number.

Scarlet O'Hara

Have you ever been to Richmond?
She asked sweetly—the scene
Before us the carnage of war,
The ruin of the South's dreams—
No, I replied—and I haven't
Been to Mecca either.

Demeter

Dawn
And the world is smeared
with a smooth gray—
a thin fine mist
hangs almost motionless
in the air
imperceptibly settling—
A twinge of sadness
when I think of her,
the image clearly visible among
the brighter shapes of my thoughts
against the grayer forms—
the twinge of sadness
one more gray shape,
not for me or for my loss
but my sadness for her—
her life
hanging motionless
like a thin fine mist
imperceptibly settling.

Hallelujah Chorus

I can get along without this
Hey, yes I can
I can get along without this
O Lord, yes I can
I was doing so before now
I can do so once again
They'll never notice I'm not here
Never know that I am gone
By the time they finally miss me
I'll be singing a whole new song
They'll never even remember me
Never recall that I was here
By the time they think of me again
It'll be this time next year
By then I'll be gone so far
Be gone so far away
Wherever it is I end up
It'll be a brand new day
I'll find myself so busy
New friends and loves and such
Whatever I have to leave behind
Won't matter all that much
I can get along without this
Hey, yes I can
I can get along without this
O Lord, yes I can.

Curved Space

I'm not thinking right
Or maybe I am
It's coming down hard
It may be a slam
Some things seem right
And some things are not
But I can't tell which
And I mostly forgot
The world lines do this
The world lines do that
And the space is all curved
The space is too fat
And one place is when
And another is where
The first one is here
The other one there
The beginning is the end
The bottom is the top
And the arrow of time
Doesn't start or stop
It doesn't come full circle
Or swing back again
You never can return
Where you've already been
And maybe I knew it
It's just hard to say
With the sun still shining
On a drab, dreary day
And some things are right
And some things are not
And I can't tell which
And I mostly forgot.

For Whom

The terrible toning of the bells
The dreary, dirgeful droning of the bells
The distant, mournful moaning of the bells
The ceaseless, grinding groaning of the bells;
And all the world is called to conclave
And all the world pauses to tell
For whom the terrible tolling of the bells.

The Coyote and the Wolves

There is an uneasy brotherhood in the wilderness—
Early in the morning we spied a coyote making its way
        hurriedly across country
A light dusting of snow on its back and shoulders, its fur
        damp and disheveled
Bent on heading straight away from whence he came;
Later we heard the howling of wolves and instantly we understood
        the coyote's concern—
For wolves kill coyotes, not for food but to rid their
        territory of them
Viewing them as competition rather than as brothers;
Where he shares with the wolf the coyote must be vigilant
Taking advantage of the bigger brother's kills but poised
        always to flee or perish.
Both are admirable canidae adapted perfectly to their surroundings
        and living by their cunning and prowess
More than enough in common, one would think, to forge a
        brotherhood
And to an extent it does; but as with all living creatures
It is an uneasy brotherhood, contingent and uncertain, fraught
        with constant danger
In which death is as natural and expected as life.

Entropy

The other day I suddenly
rediscovered a lost secret
of my youth—something
I had once done to perfection

Then somehow lost the knack
and tried for years
without success
to get it back

The fault not ineptitude
nor loss of agility
or dexterity
but a simple lack of knowledge
and understanding—

I had only lost
what was never really
mine.

The secret rediscovered—
not recapturing
my lost youth,
but the greater wisdom
and understanding
of age.

Pome: Seasons

Twin streaks of gray smitten by spring
Spiral up a tree trunk and explode
Among the barren leafless branches,
A narrow shaft of sunlight oozes
Across the wooded lot, insistent the robins
Yell out their urgency for all to hear;
A towhee scratching softly scolds
The furtive shape of a rabbit peering
From a patch of green toward the window
At the hunched form of Mr. Puff transfixed,
His tail flicking nervously, while I
Sit staring
And think of you...
(*To be continued*)

Night and Day

In the dark
I see you in his arms,
In the light
I hold you in mine;
In the dark
You found joy and delight
And promise of a love
We once shared,
In the light
I find friendship and affection
That wears only a mask of the past;
And so here we sit:
Me trapped
In the dark past,
You awakening
To the light of the future;
Is it any wonder
I fear night
And day alike?

Something New

Up
Down
And back again
Then all around
There must be some return he said
For these things that we do
They carry no assurances
Of what they mean to you
We walk, we talk
We analyze and understand
We stop short of being lovers
Though we are the best of friends
Yet nothing that we say or do
Ever seems to make amends
For what it was that led us
Up
Down
And back again
Then all around
With never any return he said
For these things that we do
We are polite and proper
You like me, I like you
But we don't dream or plan
Or try to look ahead
To see what we can see
Or find any assurances
Of what it means for me
Or what it means to you,
Till one day we will tire of this
And go in search of something new.

All Over the World

All over the world
People are dying
And I have been given another day

All over the world
People are starving
And I sit down to another meal

All over the world
People are suffering
And I lie down to peaceful slumber

All over the world
Wars, famine, poverty, sickness
And I wake up to a brave new world

All over the world
I hear them saying
You have been given another day

Use it wisely I hear them say
Use it well
You have been given another day.

A Good Day

When the arrows go right where I'm looking
Wagging neither left nor right
Flitting neither up or down
But straight to where my eyes are looking—
Then it's a good day—

When the shoulder sits secure in its seat
And the string slips smoothly from my fingers
Striking neither nose nor arm
While the bow stays stable in the hand
Pitching neither up or down
And the arrows fly straight where I'm looking—
Then it's a good day—

When the back pulls strong
With the arms relaxed
While the aim settles down
And holds steady and true
And the arrows fly straight where I'm looking—
Then it's a good day—

When the arrows bunched strike side by side
And clang and clatter against each other
And smack and smash into one another
That's all it takes—
Then it's a good day—

Do you mean these other things don't matter?
No, I mean it's a good day.

Barbarians at the Gates

Her smooth bare skin was the last symbol of civilization—
The blue-veined breasts spoke of a nurturing gentility,
But also the lust and carnal knowledge of great monuments—
Such things can be read in the turn of an ankle
The curve of a loin, the parting of beckoning lips—
These are our Phoenix: without them we are lost.

You Are That Kind of Poem

A certain kind of poem
    should be like
        a piece of music

With pleasing sounds
    or at least
        musical

And strong images
    words or notes
        not to be dismissed

Or ignored
    and silences
        to punctuate the sounds

Subtle nuance
    and themes
        over which

The composer
    labored
        to get them right

Until he did
    Beethoven's Emperor Concerto
        or Tchaikovsky's

Concerto in C
        there will be
                more than enough

In all that
        to suggest
                significant meaning

The meaning
        the music of your life
                holds for me.

Camus

Just because everything is permitted
Does not mean nothing is forbidden.

In a world where
The only certainty
Is death—
And the benign indifference of the
Universe to man—
Anything is possible
Even murder,
And nothing is important
Not even life—
And the only path to happiness
Is an utter lack
Of hope.

Sisyphus

Our bodies are not now the stout instruments
Of youth they once were—
Neither are they yet spent and impotent
With age; I suck in lungsful of the bright
New Mexico air and experience the sudden
Rush and flush of exuberance
That made me lust and love and write
Poetry; I feel alive and renewed
And know the quest is not over
But continues...

Nocturne

That which is timeless, that knows neither
The loosening of muscle and slackening of sinews
Nor the subtle decline of memory and mind—
Not the irresistible onset of age and its irrevocable reality—
But the swift vital vibrance of undiminished youth,
The healthy robust lust of flesh, tumescent and aroused,
Is what inflames my unquenchable desire for you—
Which couples us in intimate passionate embrace
Though, even apart, will sever, and sweeten, our separate slumber.

Hidden Meaning

Yes, these things are important to me, he said,
Too important not to write about them,
A smile stole slowly across each page
Woven in and out among the words;
Those things that others turn away from embarrassed—
A glance, a feeling, a sudden catch of breath—
Are to me too serious to be denied:
It's these that give a life, or a writer, meaning.

Desert Round

A bright hard
        New Mexico sun
                pours down

From azure blue
        deep desert skies
                upon the parched

And sun scoured earth
        releasing the pungent scent
                of sage along

Ancient arroyos
        amidst truncated tablelands
                dripping ochre

And burnt sienna
        down sheer sides
                straining skyward

To greet
        the bright hard
                New Mexico sun.

Fragment

Near dusk warm desert winds begin to blow,
The scent of sage and pinyon perfume the breeze,
The first stars of evening twinkle faint and yellow
Through the thin wind-swept haze,
The parched earth, pent-up and tense, relaxes
And exhales into the tranquil calm of night.

Delphi Discourse

Happiness sneaks in
Through a door you didn't know
You had left open...

Benediction

Be assured, O my friends,
Be mindful, O my foes,
That in the end
We are all human.

Self-Evaluation

I have trained the young people well—
Those eager few who have been receptive—they go on
To earn advanced degrees of their own and themselves
Become physicists and mathematicians and engineers—
Some scholars of history and philosophy and literature—
I have taught them well; though in truth nothing
Beyond to read carefully and to think for themselves
And trust their own minds. If I have taught them anything
It is to look beyond the seductive but elusive *why*
And keep their minds fixed firmly on *how* the world
Is ordered. Besides these simple truths there is no more
Exalted prescription for learning: that is merely the hype
Of hucksters and confidence-men bent on power and profit,
Or themselves bewildered and amazed at their own ignorance
And lack of understanding. Compared to such slick promises
This other way seems too simple—how is it something
So easy could work? Clearly it is not easy. Yet year after year
The young people have come and then gone away
To become scientists and scholars and artists. I have taught
Them very little, I think. Yet I have taught them well.

www.ingramcontent.com/pod-product-compliance
Lightning Source LLC
LaVergne TN
LVHW091227080426
835509LV00009B/1204